Unit Three: Communication

Being a Good Listener — 1
Written by: Bridget Gaertner & Ashley Bustamante
Illustrated by: Shaun Cochran

Talking Back and Forth — 31
Written by: Bridget Gaertner & Ashley Bustamante
Illustrated by: Shaun Cochran

Words are Important — 61
Written by: Bridget Gaertner & Ashley Bustamante
Illustrated by: Shaun Cochran

Being a Good Listener

When are times when it is important for you to be a good listener?   When can it be hard to be a good listener?

In this story, Z has a hard time listening. The kids help Z learn that it is important to be a good listener, and that you use your whole body to do that. You pay attention with your eyes and your ears, and you keep your voice quiet and your body still.

As you listen to the story, pay attention for times when Z forgets how to listen and for times when Z listens well.

One day Z spent the whole morning looking at the books in the tree house. It was so much fun to learn about new and interesting things!

Later that day, Kim and Jeremy came to the tree house and they were very excited!

"Guess what, Z?" exclaimed Jeremy. "We went to the zoo this morning and saw lots of animals! We saw…"

But before Jeremy could finish talking, Z interrupted and said, "I just looked at a book about animals, so now I know all about them! I know that monkeys can hang from their tails and penguins can slide on their tummies and flamingos can stand on one leg! Animals are awesome!"

Whoops-Z!

Z didn't know that it isn't okay to interrupt someone who is talking.

How would you tell Z to be a good listener?

"You're right, Z," agreed Kim. "Animals *are* awesome. Do you know what we saw the monkeys doing?"

But Z was gathering more books and was not looking at Kim or paying attention to what she was saying.

Whoops-Z!

Z didn't know that it's important to show someone that you're listening to them.

How would you tell Z to be a good listener?

Jeremy and Kim sat down next to Z.

"It seems like you are having a hard time listening today," they said.

Z looked puzzled. "What does that mean?"

"Well," explained Jeremy, "We listen to hear what others are saying. Everyone likes it when you listen to them."

"How do you listen?" asked Z.

The kids explained, "When you are a good listener, you look at the person with your eyes…"

"…and you listen with your ears…and you keep your voice quiet and your body still."

"But what if I really want to say something too?" asked Z.

"Well," answered Kim, "When I have to wait to talk, sometimes I cross my fingers so I remember what I want to say."

Z jumped up and down excitedly. "I want to try to be a good listener!"

"Okay, Z!" said Kim. "Let's see…we saw a huge panda bear at the zoo! It was black and white and very furry."

Z stayed still and looked at Kim while she was talking, listened very carefully and quietly, and didn't interrupt her. When she was finished talking, Z said, "Wow! Pandas sound super-duper!"

The kids cheered. "You really know how to be a good listener, Z!"

Z says,
"Whenever we're together my friends help me discover how children on earth get along with each other!"

Z wants all of you to be good listeners too!

Connecting to the Classroom

➢ **Everyday Moment:** Model respectful listening with the children in your classroom.

▸ Be explicit in describing how you are engaging in attentive listening (e.g., *I know you want to tell me something, but hold that thought for a second while I finish writing this note to myself- I want to be able to give you my full attention*).

▸ Point out the strategies you use to improve listening (e.g., *Gina, would you please move closer to Ryan? I want to make sure we can all see one another while we're talking*).

➢ **Discussions and Activities**

▸ Discuss why it is important to listen to others and how to use your whole body to listen carefully (e.g., *Look with your eyes, listen with your ears, keep your voice quiet and your body still*).

▸ Ask children to identify things that make it hard to listen and the consequences of not listening well to others.

▸ Discuss strategies to use if you forget to listen or couldn't hear or understand what someone else was saying.

▸ Have children play a version of "If You're Happy and You Know It," by replacing "happy" with "listening," and changing the actions with each verse to ensure participants are listening (e.g., *If you're listening and you know it, spin around…*).

Talking Back and Forth

If you were talking with a friend, what could happen if you both wanted to talk at the same time, all the time?

In this story, Z doesn't understand how to go back and forth when you talk to someone. The kids help Z learn how to listen and then respond, and how to take turns talking.

As you listen to the story, pay attention to what happens when Z is talking with the kids and forgets to take turns.

One afternoon Jeremy, Kim, and Z sat together in the tree house looking at books. The kids had visited the zoo and were excited to learn some more about the animals in their books.

Jeremy had a big book about reptiles. "Wow!" he said. "This book has really cool pictures of frogs and tadpoles!"

Z wondered what a tadpole was, but didn't ask.

"My book is about tigers," said Kim. "Some tigers are white instead of orange. I didn't know that—did you?"

Jeremy shook his head.

Z listened to Kim, but didn't answer.

Whoops-Z!

Z didn't know what to do after someone speaks to you.

What would you tell Z to do?

"Z, did you hear me?" asked Kim. "You're being very quiet."

Z nodded. "I'm just trying to be a good listener!"

"Oh, Z," said Kim with a smile, "You don't have to *only* listen! You get a turn to talk too!"

"I do?" asked Z.

"Sure!" said the kids. "After someone talks to you, it's nice to respond to them. That way they know that you heard them and thought about what they said."

"Can I try that?" Z asked excitedly.

"Okay, I'll start," said Kim. "My favorite animals are giraffes."

Z listened carefully and thought about what Kim had said. Then Z answered, "I like giraffes too! They have really long necks!"

Jeremy told them that his favorite animals were lions, just like the ones that were at the zoo. When Jeremy was finished, Z said, "I would like to see lions at the zoo too. And I would also like to see dolphins and flamingos and pigs and panda bears…"

Z told the kids about all the different kind of animals that Z wanted to see. Z kept talking and talking and talking……

Whoops-Z!

Z forgot to take turns talking.

What would you tell Z to do next?

The kids sat down with Z. "That was a great job listening *and* answering Jeremy," they said. "But remember that everyone gets a chance to talk. You take turns and go back and forth."

"Uh-oh!" said Z. "I forgot to give you a turn to talk!"

After that, the kids and Z gathered all of the animal books they could find and settled onto their cozy cushions. They spent the rest of the afternoon looking at books, talking back and forth, and enjoying being together.

Z says,
"Whenever we're together my friends help me discover how children on earth get along with each other!"

Z wants all of you to remember how to take turns and talk back and forth with each other too!

Connecting to the Classroom

➢ **Everyday Moment:** Explicitly reinforce children when they use reciprocal communication skills.

　▸ Highlight when children respond to one another.

　▸ Draw attention to times when children are taking turns talking.

➢ **Discussions and Activities**

　▸ Discuss what it means to *respond* to someone (e.g., *To answer someone by saying or doing something after they speak to you*) and why it is an important thing to do when someone is speaking to you.

　▸ Discuss why it is important to take turns talking and listening to others.

　▸ Have children practice listening and responding by reciting a familiar rhyme or chant, stopping at key points to fill in the missing word or phrase (e.g., *Row, row, row your ＿＿＿＿. Gently down the ＿＿＿＿).*

　▸ Have buddies roll a ball back and forth, taking turns talking about a given topic when the ball is in their possession.

　▸ Ask children whether or not it is difficult to wait for a turn to talk, and discuss strategies to use while waiting.

　▸ Divide children into two groups that face one another, and lead them in a familiar chant, having one half begin the chant and the other half respond either by repeating the words or saying the next part of the chant.

Words are
Important

Have you had a great idea that you wanted to tell someone? What did you do?

In this story, Z doesn't want to tell the kids an idea because Z is feeling shy and it doesn't seem like anyone is listening. The kids help Z learn that it's okay to speak up, because everyone has important things to say.

As you listen to the story, pay attention to what Z does when Z has an idea, and if these things worked or didn't work.

One afternoon, Mia, Kenny, and Kayla came to the tree house and were very excited! They had a big, colorful box with something new inside!

"Look at this!" said Mia. "It's a bubble machine! It blows bubbles out of all these different tubes."

Z didn't know anything about bubbles, but this sure looked exciting! Z and the kids scrambled to pull all of the pieces out of the box.

"How do we put it together?" wondered Kenny. "There are no instructions!"

The kids and Z decided to look at the picture on the box, and then they worked together until they made the bubble machine look just the same as the picture.

"I wonder how we turn it on," said Kayla.

The kids and Z looked at the bubble machine and did not know what to do.

Suddenly, Z saw a little green button that looked like it might work! But Z didn't say anything because Z was afraid of having the wrong idea.

The kids tried to figure out how to turn on the bubble machine.

Finally, Z pointed toward the green button, but no one saw.

Then Z said, very softly, "I think I know what to do." But no one responded.

Now Z didn't want to say anything else. Z thought the kids didn't really want to listen to what Z had to say.

Whoops-Z!

Z forgot that we can speak up when we have things to say.

What do you think Z should do next?

Kayla asked why Z was being so quiet.

"I might know how to turn on the bubble machine," Z answered. "But I don't think anyone wants to hear my idea."

"Everyone has important things to say, Z!" said Kayla. "Sometimes we might not hear you or we might not understand what you're trying to say. That's when you can try to speak up again in a different way."

"But, when I tried AGAIN, no one listened!" said Z.

"Well," said Kenny, "When you want to say something you can also use a nice, strong voice."

"But what if I don't have a very good idea?" Z wondered.

"That's okay!" said Mia. "Everyone's ideas are important. Sometimes they don't work but they are still important to share."

"I HAVE AN IDEA!" shouted Z.

The kids laughed, "Z, that voice is TOO strong! Try that voice again more softly, so you can speak up but also speak kindly."

Z looked at the kids, used a nice, strong voice that wasn't TOO loud, and said, "I saw a green button on the bubble machine. I think that's how we can turn it on."

Kayla pushed the green button, and it worked! Now there were bubbles everywhere!

Kayla, Kenny, Mia, and Z had so much fun chasing and popping bubbles together all afternoon!

Z says,
"Whenever we're together my friends help me discover how children on earth get along with each other!"

Z wants all of you to remember that when you have something to say, it is important to speak up.

Connecting to the Classroom

➢ **Everyday Moment:** Encourage children to speak up in everyday moments.

   ▸ Reinforce children for speaking assertively.

   ▸ Provide support for those who may be more passive or reluctant to speak up in a group.

➢ **Discussions and Activities**

   ▸ Ask children to think of situations in which it would be important to speak up.

   ▸ Discuss what to do if you tried to speak up and no one heard you.

   ▸ Discuss what it means to "speak up and speak kindly".

   ▸ Have children take turns speaking assertively into a *microphone* about a given topic.